Dakota

I0500403

*Tallgrass Prairie
Habitat Preservation Area
Environmental Assessment*

Environmental Assessment

Dakota

Tallgrass Prairie Habitat

Preservation Area

Prepared by:

U.S. Fish and Wildlife Service
Sand Lake National Wildlife Refuge
39650 Sand Lake Drive
Columbia, SD 57433

and

U.S. Fish and Wildlife Service
Refuges and Wildlife, Division of Realty
134 Union Blvd., Suite 350
Lakewood, CO 80228-1807

January 2000

Table of Contents

Chapter 4. Environmental Consequences

Chapter 5. Coordination and Environmental Review

Appendices

Figure

Chapter 1.
Purpose of and Need for Action

Introduction and Background

Since 1958, the U.S. Fish and Wildlife Service (Service) has been protecting waterfowl breeding habitat that includes wetlands and upland habitats in the Prairie Pothole Region of South Dakota. The Service has been protecting habitat in fee title and easement as Waterfowl Production Areas (WPAs) using Migratory Bird Conservation Funds under the Authority of the Migratory Bird Conservation Act. The Service has always recognized the significant and diverse wildlife values associated with the Prairie Pothole Region.

The eastern portion of the Prairie Pothole Region of South Dakota is part of the tallgrass prairie ecoregion. In the United States, less than 1 percent of the tallgrass prairie remains. It is estimated that in the Dakota's, less than 9 percent of the original tallgrass prairie remains unplowed. The tallgrass prairie supports a rich variety of plant, animal, and insect species. Many of these are endemic only to the tallgrass prairie, and many are now in decline and some are listed as threatened or endangered.

The traditional Service easement and fee title protection used in the tallgrass prairie area of South Dakota focus on protecting habitat for breeding waterfowl due to the nature of the funding source for these programs. While many of these WPAs and grassland easements protect tallgrass prairie, they were not acquired for that purpose but for the wetland quality. Additionally, remaining tracts of tallgrass prairie with insufficient wetland complexes do not qualify for these programs.

In 1995, the Service officially identified the need to protect the remaining northern tallgrass prairie in North and South Dakota with the approval of the "Preliminary Project Proposal Northern Tallgrass Prairie Project, North Dakota—South Dakota" as identified in Preliminary Project Proposal. This project calls for a creation of a Habitat Preservation Area (HPA) boundary of approximately 140,860 acres for the protection of tallgrass prairie in South Dakota, primarily through the purchase of grassland easements.

This document addresses the U.S. Fish and Wildlife Service's proposal to protect tallgrass prairie in northeastern Brown County in South Dakota through the use of grassland easements purchased with Land and Water Conservation Funding.

Proposed Action

The proposed project seeks to protect a maximum 5,000 acres of remaining native prairie within the 140,860-acre boundary of the Tallgrass Prairie Habitat Preservation Area within the region of northeast Brown County, South Dakota. Protection of the prairie will be accomplished primarily through acquisition of perpetual grassland easements from willing sellers. Fee title transfer and restoration activity may also be conducted. Approximately 20 landowners would be involved at a cost of $2 million over 10 years. The funding is provided by the Land and Water Conservation Fund. Monies from this fund are derived primarily from oil and gas leases on the outer continental shelf, excess motorboat fuel tax revenues, and sale of surplus Federal property.

Purpose of and Need for Proposed Action

The purpose of the proposed action is to: 1) protect remaining tracts of tallgrass prairie from conversion to cropland, 2) protect habitat for wildlife and plants that they use and are dependent upon within the tallgrass prairie region, and 3) promote ecosystem management in order to maintain, sustain, and enhance the historic plant, animal, and insect biodiversity of native prairie habitats.

Project Area

The project area is the northeastern six townships of Brown County, South Dakota. These townships are Hecla, Portage, North Detroit, Lansing, Shelby, and South Detroit.

This area is approximately 220 square miles in extent. The dominate soils of the project area are primarily sandy soils of the Serden-Hamar-Venlo and Embden-Hecla-Ulen associates.

The project area is predominately in private ownership used for cattle grazing and hay production. The smaller unbroken prairie tracts of the area are essentially islands of relict tallgrass prairie in the midst of almost continuous cropland. These tallgrass prairie relicts, particularly in areas of lower relief described as sandy tallgrass transition prairie, are rapidly being leveled or tilled and converted to cropland. Public land is primarily owned by the Service (Refuges, Waterfowl Production Areas) and the State of South Dakota (State school land).

Decisions to be Made

Based on the analysis provided in this Environmental Assessment, the Regional Director of the U.S. Fish and Wildlife Service, Region 6 - Mountain Prairie Region, will make three decisions.

1. Determine whether the Service should establish a boundary of the Tallgrass Prairie Habitat Preservation Area of Brown County, South Dakota. If yes,
2. Select an alternate method of protecting the tallgrass prairie in the project area.
3. Determine whether the selected alternative will have a significant impact upon the quality of the human environment. This decision is required by the National Environmental Policy Act (NEPA) of 1969. If the quality of the human environment is not affected, a Finding of No Significant Impact (FONSI) will be signed and will be made available to the public. If the alternative will have a significant impact, then an Environmental Impact Statement (EIS) will be prepared to further address those impacts. If the Regional Director's decision is to establish the Tallgrass Prairie Habitat Preservation Area of Brown County, South Dakota, he will formally declare his decision by signing a Decision Document.

Issues Identified and Selected for Analysis

A scoping meeting was conducted on April 7, 1999, to receive comments from the public on issues and concerns regarding the proposed establishment of the Tallgrass Prairie Habitat Preservation Area of Brown County, South Dakota. Eleven people attended this meeting. Most attendants were there primarily to learn about the proposal. Few comments were made.

Service representatives also met with the Brown County Commissioners and local representatives for each of South Dakota's Senators and the Congressman.

During the scoping period, the Service received no written comments concerning the proposed project.

Based on the few verbal comments received, the Service identified biological, social, and economic concerns. This EA focuses on biological issues related to protection of grassland and upland habitat, rare and sensitive plants and wildlife species: social and economic issues related to landownership and uses, property taxes, and long-term impacts on rural lifestyles.

Biological Issues
Wildlife Habitat Protection
The loss of tallgrass prairie to agricultural conversion has been identified as a primary threat by the Service to the tallgrass ecosystem of South Dakota. The Service seeks to establish a Tallgrass Prairie Habitat Preservation Area to protect the remaining tracts of tallgrass prairie to provide habitat for the plants and wildlife use. The proposed project would also protect the biological diversity of the area.

Social and Economic Issues
Landownership/Land Use
The Service has been contacted by many landowners who support the project and are interested in enrolling their land in the easement program. A few individuals felt the project boundary should be extended to include more landowners, specifically to the east of the project area.

Issues Not Selected
One individual expressed concern regarding control of noxious weeds on the project sites.

Since this is primarily an easement program, the land enrolled in the program does not change ownership and, therefore, the control of noxious weeds would remain the responsibility of the landowner.

One individual expressed concern about the projects impact on property tax. Since this is primarily an easement program, the land enrolled in the program does not change hands and, therefore, the taxes paid by the landowner are not effected.

One individual asked if the Service had considered less than perpetual easements. The purpose of the proposed project is to protect remaining tracts of tallgrass prairie. Less than perpetual easements would not meet this need.

Related Actions And Activities

Natural Resources Conservation Service (NRCS) offers several programs for conservation of habitat and resources in the project area. The Conservation Reserve Program provides payments to landowners to retire cropland and restore grassland vegetative cover for a period of at least 10 years. Approximately 6,000 acres of land in the project area are enrolled in the Conservation Reserve Program (CRP). NRCS also offers the Wetland Reserve Program which provides payments to restore wetlands and adjacent uplands for 30 years to perpetuity. Approximately 1,500 acres of land in the project area are enrolled in the Wetland Reserve Program.

South Dakota Department of Game, Fish, and Parks (SDGF&P) manages over 4,700 acres of State Wildlife Development Area lands within the project area. Few, if any, of these acres appear to be native prairie.

National Wildlife Refuge System and Authorities

The Service proposes to protect lands within the project area through conservation easements to enhance the survival prospects of endangered and threatened species in the area, and to protect and maintain grassland and wetland habitat for migratory birds and other species of animals and plants. The proposed resource protection actions would be consistent with the mission and guiding principles for the management and general public use of the National Wildlife Refuge System.

Guiding Principles of the National Wildlife Refuge System

1. **Habitat.** Fish and wildlife will not prosper without high-quality habitat, and without fish and wildlife, traditional uses of refuges cannot be sustained. The Refuge System will continue to conserve and enhance the quality and diversity of fish and wildlife habitat within refuges.
2. **Public Use.** The Refuge System provides important opportunities for compatible wildlife-dependent recreational activities involving hunting, fishing, wildlife observation and photography, and environmental education and interpretation.
3. **Partnership.** America's sportsmen and women were the first partners who insisted on protecting valuable wildlife habitat within national wildlife refuges. Conservation partnership with other Federal agencies, State agencies, Tribes, organizations, industry and the general public can make significant contributions to the growth and management of the Refuge System.
4. **Public Involvement.** The public should be given full and open opportunity to participate in decisions regarding acquisition and management of our National Wildlife Refuges.

The Conservation Easement Program through the tallgrass prairie in northeast South Dakota would be administered as part of the Refuge System and operated under a Habitat Preservation Area in accordance with the overall mission of the National Wildlife Refuge System. The mission of the National Wildlife Refuge System is to "preserve a national network of lands and waters for the conservation and management of fish, wildlife, and plant resources of the United States for the benefit of present and future generations." The broad goals of the National Wildlife Refuge System describe the conservation of the nation's wildlife resources for the ultimate benefit of people.

Goals of the National Wildlife Refuge System

A. To preserve, restore, and enhance in their natural ecosystems (when practicable) all species of animals and plants that are endangered or threatened with becoming endangered.

B. To perpetuate the migratory bird resource.

C. To preserve a natural diversity and abundance of fauna and flora on refuge lands.

D. To provide an understanding and appreciation of fish and wildlife ecology and the human's role in the environment.

E. To provide refuge visitors with high-quality, safe, wholesome and enjoyable recreational experiences oriented toward wildlife, to the extent these activities are compatible with the purpose for which the refuge was established.

The proposed Tallgrass Prairie Habitat Preservation Area would be managed as part of the National Wildlife Refuge System in accordance with the National Wildlife Refuge System Administration Act of 1966, Refuge Recreation Act of 1962, Executive Order 12996 (Management and General Public Use of the National Wildlife Refuge System), National Wildlife Refuge System Improvement Act of 1997, and other relevant legislation, executive orders, regulations and policies.

Conservation of additional wildlife habitat in the tallgrass prairie area would also continue to be consistent with the following policies and management plans:

1. Prairie Pothole Joint Venture (PPJV 1987, 1994 updated)
2. North American Waterfowl Management Plan (USFWS 1994)
3. Peregrine Falcon Recovery Plan (USFWS 1984)
4. Bald Eagle Recovery Plan (Northern states) (USFWS 1983)
5. Whooping Crane Recovery Plan (USFWS 1994 revised)
6. Neotropical Migratory Bird Conservation Initiative (USFWS 1990)
7. Western Hemisphere Shorebird Reserve Network (USFWS 1985)
8. Multi-Agency Approach To Planning and Evaluation Waterfowl Management Plan for the Sand Lake Wetland Management District (USFWS 1995)

The Habitat Protection and Land Acquisition Process

Once a project area boundary is approved, various means could be used for habitat protection through the purchase of fee title or conservation easements, no-cost transfer, long-term lease, donation or exchange. It is the established policy of the Service to acquire land or interest of land from willing sellers.

The authorities for the acquisition of the proposed Tallgrass Prairie Habitat Preservation Area are the Fish and Wildlife Act of 1956 (16 U.S.C. 742 f (b) (1), as amended and the Refuge Recreation Act of 1969 (16 U.S.C. 460k-460k-4), as amended. Acquisition funding is made available through the Land and Water Conservation Fund Act of 1965. The Federal monies used to acquire conservation easements on private lands through the Land and Water Conservation Fund are derived primarily from oil and gas leases on the outer continental shelf, excess motorboat fuel tax revenues, and sale of surplus Federal property. Additional funds could be made available through Congressional appropriations, Natural Resources Conservation Service's Wetland Reserve Program, or other sources to acquire lands, waters, or interest therein for fish and wildlife conservation purposes.

The basic considerations in acquiring land are the biological significance of the land, existing and anticipated threats to wildlife resources, and landowner's willingness to sell or otherwise make property available to the project. The purchase of conservation easements proceeds according to availability of funds.

Although it is the intent of the Service to mainly purchase conservation easements as a type of habitat protection for this project, other various means could be used for habitat protection through fee title purchase, no-cost transfers, long-term leases, donations, and exchanges. Under provisions of the Refuge Revenue Sharing Act (Public Law 95-469), the Service would annually reimburse counties to offset revenue lost as a result of acquisition of private property in fee title. This Law states that the Secretary of the Interior (Secretary) shall pay to each county in which any area acquired in fee title is situated, the greater of the following amounts:

1. An amount equal to the product of 75 cents multiplied by the total acreage of that portion of the fee area which is located within such county.
2. An amount equal to ¾ of 1 percent of the fair market value, as determined by the Secretary, for that portion of the fee area which is located within such county.
3. An amount equal to 25 percent of the net receipts collected by the Secretary in connection with the operation and management of such fee area during such fiscal year. However, if a fee area is located in two or more counties, the amount for each county shall be apportioned in relationship to the acreage in that county.

The Refuge Revenue Sharing Act also requires that Service lands be reappraised every five years to ensure that payments to local governments remain equitable. Payments under this Act would be made only on lands that the Service acquires in fee title. On lands where the Service acquires only partial interest through easement, all taxes would remain the responsibility of the individual landowner.

Chapter 2.
Alternatives, Including The Preferred Alternative

Chapter 2 describes the two alternatives identified for this project: 1) a no-action alternative and 2) an alternative giving the Service the authority to create the Tallgrass Prairie Habitat Preservation Area, a grassland easement program in the northeast corner of South Dakota. The no-action alternative considers the effect of not establishing a conservation easement program within the project area boundary identified in the EA. The effects of the action alternative (preferred alternative) establishing the Tallgrass HPA are also considered.

If the preferred alternative is selected, current and future conservation easements acquired by the U.S. Fish and Wildlife Service will be administered in accordance with Executive Order 12996, Management and General Public Use of The National Wildlife Refuge System (1996) and the National Wildlife Refuge System Improvement Act (1997). Management activities would include monitoring the properties to ensure that landowners did not violate the terms of the easement. The Service would continue to monitor the status and recovery of endangered, threatened and candidate species, conduct other activities for enhancing wildlife habitat and restoring native species with landowners permission and coordinate with private organizations, and State and Federal agencies.

Alternative A. No-Action

Under the No-Action alternative, the Tallgrass Prairie Habitat Preservation Area would not be established and, therefore, funds from the Land and Water Conservation fund would not be used to purchase perpetual grassland easements in the project area. Native prairie grasslands in the 140,680-acre study area would continue to be vulnerable to conversion to cropland as the agricultural economy changes or when the land changes ownership. Grassland easements would still be available through proceeds from the Migratory Bird Commission (Duck Stamps) that are associated with wetlands, grants from the North American Waterfowl Conservation Act, and cooperatives with non-profit organizations.

Alternative B. Establish the Tallgrass Prairie Habitat Preservation Area

Under Alternative B, the Service would establish a grassland conservation easement program with Land and Water Conservation Funds in the northeast corner of South Dakota. Within the 140,860-acre project, approximately 5,000 acres of grasslands would be perpetually protected. Priority areas for purchasing easements would be high-quality native prairie that is also high-quality habitat for waterfowl, nongame migratory birds, and other wildlife. Grasslands, or land in lower priority zones with other types of cover, may be purchased to connect and round-out larger tracts of high-quality grasslands (see Figure 1).

The easement program would rely on voluntary participation from landowners. Grazing would not be restricted on the land under the easement contract, although haying would be restricted until after July 15th and cultivating the land would not be permitted. All land would remain in private ownership, therefore, property tax, weed control responsibilities, and control of public access to the land would not change.

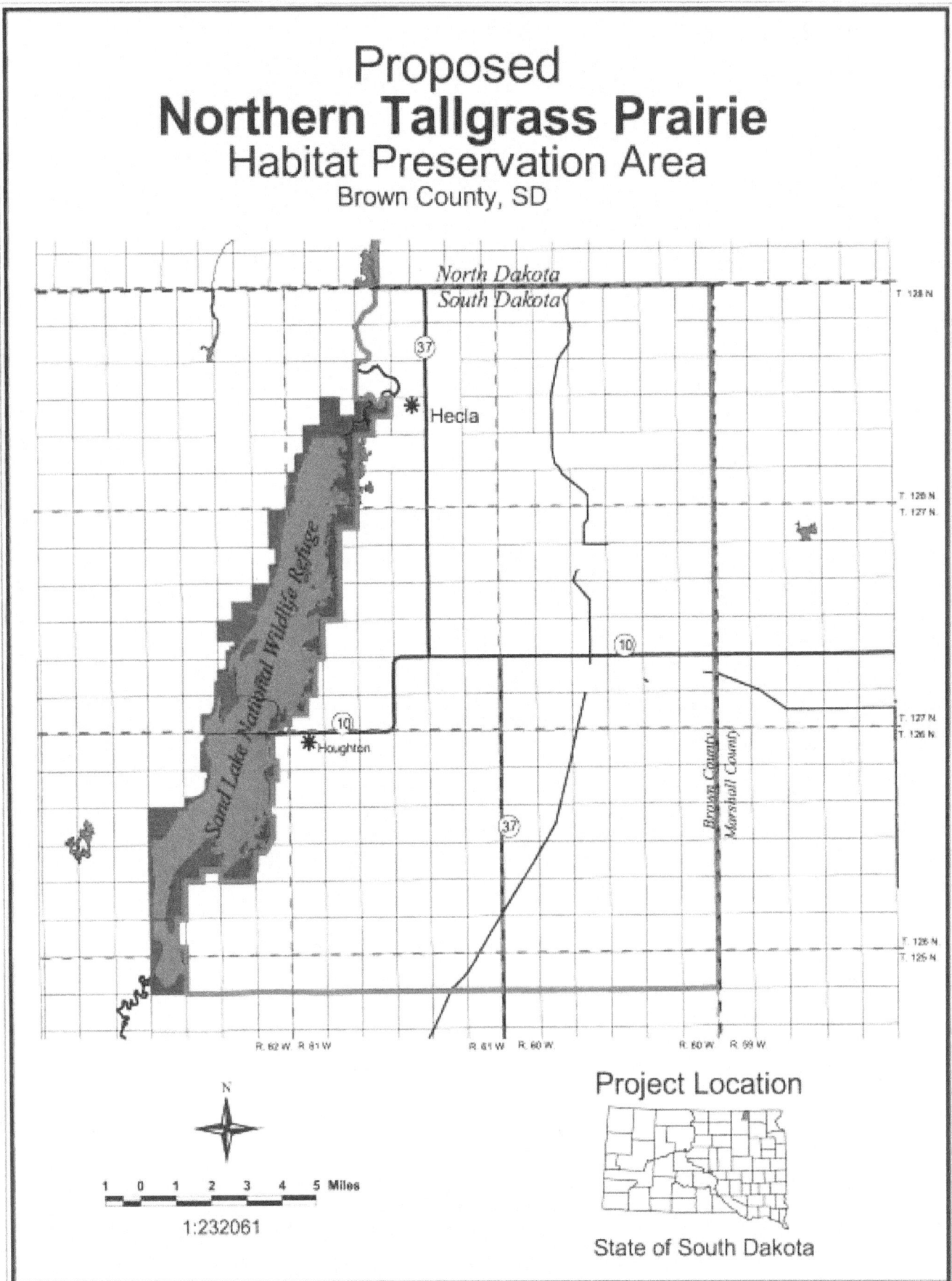

Proposed
Northern Tallgrass Prairie
Habitat Preservation Area
Brown County, SD

Project Location

State of South Dakota

Figure 1.

Chapter 3.
Affected Environment

This Chapter describes the existing biological, social, and economic resources that would most likely be affected by this project.

Biological Environment

Historically, the landscape of this area consisted of a large grassland ecosystem dotted with numerous marshes closely associated with groundwater and possibly highly influenced by flows in the James River that forms the west boundary of the area.

During the last century, the grasslands have been largely converted to intensively cultivated cropland. Portions of the area were drained in the early 1900's by an extensive system called the Crow Creek Drain. Most of these ditches in the project area are not functional or minimally functional at the present time and have been legally abandoned.

Due to the sandy nature of the soils, high water table, and density of wetlands within the project area, portions have remained relatively undisturbed by agriculture and are primarily used for native hayland or rangeland. In recent years, however, significant new threats to the area have appeared and conversion of grassland to cropland has gained renewed interest.

Due to recent advances in no-till and minimum-till farming, irrigation using groundwater, and the production of specialty crops (potatoes, carrots, onions, etc.), the remaining native prairie in this area has come under considerable pressure to be converted. In recent years, thousands of acres of this region located across the border in North Dakota have been converted to potato farming by using heavy equipment to level the land and center pivot irrigation installed. This practice not only destroys the native prairie on the land being converted, but as some area farmers and ranchers fear, the use of the shallow groundwater table for irrigation will lower water levels on the adjacent shallow wetlands and subirrigated meadows thereby destroying them.

The Service has documented several cases in the past several years where portions of the native prairie in the project area have been converted to cropland. Increased taxation of the land has been a factor in South Dakota as well as the advances of farming technology. An Environmental Assessment (USFWS, 1994) recently completed by the Service stated that "The remaining tracts of native prairie (in the project area) are probably the rarest types of remaining prairie within the Wetland Management District (eight county area) and have the greatest probability of conversion (to farm land)."

In 1991, the Service initiated the grassland easement program. This program uses money derived from the sale of Duck Stamps to purchase perpetual easements on private lands that have high waterfowl breeding pair densities. These easements protect the grasslands with associated wetlands in perpetuity. The grasslands protected by the easement must remain as grass; they may be hayed only after July 15 of each year. Grazing is not restricted.

In July 1995, Brown County landowners in the project area were contacted by the Service informing them of a variety of programs that would be available to protect the native prairie on land they own. The landowners were selected using the technology developed by the Service which showed that they owned land with high waterfowl production potential.

The response from the letter sent to landowners has been very good. To date, options have been signed to place grassland easements on over 7,500 acres of grassland in the "sandhills" portion of the project area. Approximately 15,500 acres of native prairie are present.

Some of the remaining native prairie located in the project area has low wetland densities making it more difficult to justify spending Duck Stamp dollars to protect this unique prairie. The proposed project will make it possible to purchase easements for the purpose of protecting these prairie tracts that do not qualify for existing programs.

Habitat

In northeastern Brown County and northwestern Marshall County, South Dakota, a very unique and relatively small grassland ecosystem exists. The soils of this grassland are dominated by the Hecla-Hamar-Ullen association which is nearly level to undulating, well-drained to poorly drained, sandy and loamy soils (USDA. SCS 1936).

Portions of this area have a very rough topography with a high density of wetlands, and blowouts occur in the choppy hills. Soils of this area are classified as the Maddock-Serden and the Serden-Hamar-Venlo associations which are excessively drained, somewhat poorly drained, and poorly drained level to rolling, sandy soils on glacial plains. This area is referred to by the local communities as the "Hecla Sandhills." Much of the Sandhills remains in grass, and the majority of the grass is native prairie.

These sandy soils have evolved a grassland ecosystem which is very unusual to this region. This grassland ecosystem is considered to be a Sandy Tallgrass Transition Prairie (STTP) dominated by plants such as big bluestem, sand bluestem, prairie sandreed, needle-and-thread, green needlegrass, Indiangrass, and western wheatgrass. See Appendix A for species listed in this document with accompanying scientific names.

The vegetation of the Hecla Sandhills is mapped as Nebraska Sandhills prairie. The nearest extent of the Nebraska Sandhills lies some 200 miles south-southwest of the Hecla Sandhills in extreme south-central South Dakota, distinguishing the Hecla Sandhills as an extreme outlier of this vegetation type. The closest area of other substantial sandhills topography and vegetation approaches only 50 miles to the northeast as the Sheyenne National Grassland of southeastern North Dakota, but the slightly higher precipitation there supports oak savanna type vegetation.

The Hecla Sandhills area is surrounded by a more level to gently undulating topography which has a very high water table. This area has numerous subirrigated meadows that are used as native hayland and pasture. The majority of this area has been converted to cropland; however, some relatively large tracts (greater than 160 acres) of native prairie remain. The entire region covers approximately 220 square miles in South Dakota with less than 25 square miles considered to be Sandhills.

Wetlands

The Service has recently developed technology using GIS (Geographic Information System) and the National Wetland Inventory which enables the identification of areas with high potential for waterfowl production. This technology has identified the Sandhills portion of the project area as ranking in the top 2 of 1 percent in northeastern and northcentral South Dakota for its potential for waterfowl production due to its exceptional wetland complex.

Two 4-square mile plots located in this area have been surveyed annually since 1989 for breeding waterfowl. This has been done as a result of the Multi-Agency Approach to Planning and Evaluation process (MAAPE) conducted by Habitat and Population Evaluation Team (HAPET) located in Bismarck, North Dakota. Results of this study indicate that the two plots have recruitment rates of .61 and .51. Each of these rates exceed the minimum set for managed areas in the Prairie Pothole Joint Venture Plan (PPJV), and the .61 rate exceeds the established rate in the primary objective of the plan.

The project area is located within the United States portion of the Prairie Pothole Region which is the focus area of the PPJV.

Due to the high density of wetlands in the project area, breeding habitat is available for many other wetland dependent birds. Some examples known to occur in the area are: marsh wrens, sedge wrens, marbled godwits, willets, phalaropes, yellowthroats, black terns, and many other nongame species.

Uplands

The grassland ecosystem in the project area is not found anywhere else in South Dakota except a small portion of the Nebraska sandhills in south-central South Dakota. Even though these two areas are similar, differences do exist. This habitat supports a variety of grassland dependent birds such as song sparrows, chestnut-collared longspurs, savannah sparrows, grasshopper sparrows, bobolinks, and many others.

The Hecla Sandhills area of Brown and Marshall Counties is still dominated by native prairie, while scattered tracts of the flatter portions of the project area surrounding the Sandhills remain in native prairie. These are the subirrigated meadows and areas with high water tables.

Agriculture dominates the landscape for miles in all directions around the project area where little or no native prairie remains. The project area is literally an island in a sea of agriculture.

Floristic surveys conducted during 1996 and 1997 identified 411 vascular plant species representing 75 families (Fairlee). Three of these, pinweed, sedge, and Prairie Dunewort, were documented for the first time in South Dakota. Other species of interest were prairie loosestrife, found only in South Dakota in the Hecla Sandhills, and moonwort, previously only documented once in Lawrence County, South Dakota in the Black Hills. Other species monitored by the State Heritage Program and found in the area include alpine rush, meadowsweet, and Great Plains ladies'-tresses. In addition, grass-leaved rush and a paspalum were discovered, both representing significant northward range extensions from the Nebraska Sandhills.

The project area is also suitable habitat for the endangered western prairie fringed orchid. Surveys conducted in 1985, 1996, and 1997 found none.

Plants monitored by the South Dakota Natural Heritage database which might occur or that have been documented in the Hecla Sandhills are as follows:

Western Prairie Fringed Orchid	Prairie Dunewort
Smooth Goosefoot	Alpine Rush
Prairie Loosestrife	Meadowsweet
Nodding Ladies Tresses	

Maps depicting the historic range of the northern tallgrass prairie show the project area falls just outside of the western boundary. However, the floristic surveys conducted in 1996 and 1997 show that the project area is dominated by species which are used as indicator of true tallgrass prairie. These include big bluestem, porcupine grass, little bluestem, Indian grass, prairie cordgrass and associated forbs like lead plant, Maximillian's sunflower and prairie coneflower. While the project area on some maps is shown in a mixed grass/tallgrass transition zone, the survey indicates that it fits well with the tallgrass prairie designation (personal communications with Gary Larson).

Less than 2 percent of the original tallgrass prairie remain making it one of the rarest and most fragmented North American ecosystems.

Wildlife

The Dakota skipper, which is a candidate species for Federal listing under the Endangered Species Act, is found in the project area. This species is considered rare in South Dakota. This species requires relatively undisturbed native tallgrass and mid-grass prairie. Also known to occur in the area is the regal fritillary. Other butterfly species monitored by the South Dakota Natural Heritage database that might occur in the area are listed below.

Scientific Name	Common Name	Status and Rank
Atrytone arogos iowa	Iowa Skipper	Monitored Species G4 T4 S2
Hesperia ottoe	Ottoe Skipper	Monitored Species G3 S2
Oarisma powesheik	Powesheik Skipperling	Monitored Species G3 S3

Within the project area exists a small but viable population of greater prairie chickens. These prairie chickens are primarily found in and adjacent to the Sandhills. No other significant numbers of prairie chickens are known to occur in northeast South Dakota or southeast North Dakota. The nearest viable population of prairie chickens is found in the Sheyenne grasslands of North Dakota, and this population is in decline.

Social and Economic Considerations

The rural communities of Houghton and Hecla are located within the project area. Hecla's population is estimated at 400 and Houghton's populations is much smaller. Farming and cattle ranching are the main economic practices within the area. Many of the local residents commute to Aberdeen or Britton for employment. Big game and waterfowl hunting are the most popular activities in the fall. While Sand Lake National Wildlife Refuge does not lie within the project area, it does lie directly adjacent to the area and consequently provides the local area with economic benefits derived from its many visitors. An estimated 18,000 people visit the Refuge each year to observe wildlife and participate in its hunting and fishing opportunities.

Agricultural Resources

Agricultural practices in the project area are intense. The majority of the area is intensively farmed, producing wheat, corn, soybeans, and to a lesser degree, sunflowers and alfalfa.

Land that is not farmed is primarily used for cattle pasture. Many of these pastures have previous farming histories and were converted back to grass due to the sandy nature of the soil or wet conditions.

Landownership

This project will not impact landownership. The use of grassland easements does not change the ownership of the land.

Property Tax

Property tax on private land is currently paid to the counties by the landowner. Since acquisition of easements does not result in a transfer of land title, private landowners would continue to pay property taxes. If the Service does purchase any fee title acquisitions, the affected counties would receive mitigated payments from the Service in lieu of property taxes under the Refuge Revenue Sharing Act (see Chapter 1).

Public Use and Wildlife-Dependent Recreational Activities

Under this proposal, all land will stay in private ownership. The proposed easements do not impact the landowners ability to control access to the land by hunters, fishermen, and trappers.

This proposal will not impact public use or wildlife-dependent recreational activities.

Cultural Resources

The U.S. Fish and Wildlife Service, as a Federal agency, has a trust responsibility to Tribes which includes the protection of the sovereignty of the Tribal government and preservation of Tribal culture and other trust resources. The easement program does not compromise Tribal jurisdiction or Tribal rights because it deals only with willing sellers of private land for an easement. The protection of trust resources is enhanced with the easement program by conservation of wildlife habitat and protection of resources from land conversion and development.

Archaeological and historical resources within any fee title would receive protection under Federal laws mandating the management and protection of cultural resources. These laws include, but are not limited to, the Archaeological Resources Protection Act, the Archaeological and Historic Preservation Act, the Native American Graves Protection and Repatriation Act, Native American Religion Freedom Act, and the National Historic Preservation Act.

Currently, the Service does not propose any project, activity, or program that would result in changes in the character of, or would potentially adversely affect any historic cultural resource or archaeological site. When such undertakings are considered, the Service would take all necessary steps to comply with Section 106 of the National Historic Preservation Act (NHPA) of 1966, as amended. The Service would also pursue proactive compliance with Section 110 of the NHPA to survey, inventory, and evaluate cultural resources.

This proposal will have no impact on cultural resources. The project may help to preserve cultural resources by prohibiting grasslands from being converted to farmland.

Contaminants and Hazardous Wastes

Fieldwork for the contaminant survey will be conducted prior to the purchase of land interest. The preliminary survey will be conducted on these properties to determine if contaminants pose a threat to fish and wildlife or if they would be a liability to the Service. The Contaminants Coordinator located at Ecological Services Office, Pierre, South Dakota or qualified personnel from the Wetland Acquisition Office in Aberdeen, South Dakota will be contacted to ensure policies and guidelines are followed before acquisition.

Chapter 4.
Environmental Consequences

Effects on the Biological Environment
This section assesses the environmental impacts expected to occur from the implementation of Alternatives A or B as described in Chapter 2. Environmental impacts are analyzed by issues for each alternative and appear in the same order as discussed in Chapter 1.

Wildlife Habitat Protection
Alternative A (No-Action):
Without the perpetual protection from easements created through the Tallgrass Prairie Project, the future of grasslands in the project area would be uncertain.

Additional losses of grasslands may contribute to the long-term decline in nest success for upland nesting wildlife species. Most upland species avoid nesting in cropland. It is likely that predation would continue to be a major reason for nest loss in waterfowl and other upland nesting birds since each additional conversion of grassland to cropland would create islands of grass easily searched by predators (Cowardin et al. 1985, Sovada et al. 1995). If grasslands were not protected with easements and converted to cropland, high quality nesting habitat could be restored by planting cover (cool season grasses/forbs). Other intensive management techniques such as predator control, fencing exclosures, and artificial nesting islands also could be used (Beauchamp et al. 1996). While all of these measures may be beneficial to overall nest success, they are significantly more expensive than easements, and none of them would completely recreate native prairie.

If additional prairie habitat were tilled, several species of grassland birds that are restricted to this type of habitat would be negatively affected. Cultivated land is considered unsuitable nesting habitat for these species (Owens and Myers 1972). A reduction in nesting habitat may mean that the tallgrass prairie would no longer be an area of relatively high grassland bird density, and populations in the project area may begin to decline as they have in other parts of their ranges (Breeding Bird Survey 1966-1996). Some of these species may have to receive special protection from the Endangered Species Act if their populations continue to decline.

Conversion of grassland to cropland would increase the pesticide load on the environment. The effects of pesticides on wildlife are estimated to be high and could include reduction of nesting cover for birds, direct contamination of egg embryos, and losses in the aquatic invertebrate food base critical for many nesting birds, particularly waterfowl (Dwernychuk and Boag 1973, Pimentel et al. 1992).

Alternative B (Preferred):

Establishing the 140,680-acre Tallgrass Prairie HPA would protect up to 5,000 acres of native prairie to be protected in perpetuity. This would help maintain the uniqueness of the tallgrass prairie within South Dakota as an area of relatively intact grasslands that harbor a wide variety of wildlife species. These 5,000 acres would complement other Service easement programs and existing public grasslands such as waterfowl production areas and state wildlife management areas, allowing for the preservation of a network of grasslands in the project area. These areas of protected grasslands would exist regardless of changes in agricultural policy or economy, which are known to affect the rate of grassland conversion (Gerard 1995).

Purchasing grassland easements within the project boundary would prevent the conversion of grasslands, where nest success for waterfowl is higher, to cropland where nest success is lower (Klett *et al.* 1988). Other species of upland nesting birds also have higher nest success rates in grasslands than in cropland (Kantrud and Higgins 1992). Thus, protecting the relatively intact grasslands in the project area represents a significant opportunity for maintaining wildlife species populations throughout the tallgrass prairie region.

Protecting grasslands in the project area would help maintain the ability of the tallgrass prairie to act as a buffer against population declines grassland birds are experiencing in other parts of their ranges. Long-term prospects for grassland birds are considered poor (Sauer *et al.* 1995). Preserving grasslands in this portion of their range may prevent some of these species from needing protection from the Endangered Species Act.

Protected grasslands would also act as buffers for wetlands near cropland treated with pesticides by filtering up to 70 percent of runoff (Hartwig and Hall 1980). This may reduce the impact on wildlife (i.e., nesting ducks) from ingesting contaminated invertebrates and/or the loss of the invertebrate food base due to die-offs caused by pesticides (Grue *et al.* 1988, Kantrud *et al.* 1989).

Effects on Social and Economic Issues
Landownership/Land use
Alternative A (No-Action):

If the Tallgrass Prairie Project was not established, far fewer perpetual grassland easements would be created. Fewer acres in the project area permanently restricted from conversion to cropland would exist. As the economy changed or land was sold, the use of the land could be changed. The resale value of fewer properties would be affected by easements.

Without the easement program, the Service may consider fee title purchases more often. This would limit the total number of acres the Service could protect for wildlife habitat since fee title lands cost three to four times as much as easements and require more time to process. These purchases would probably be limited to landowners with large tracts of prairie for sale and/or land adjacent to waterfowl production areas and national wildlife refuges in order to maximize the wildlife benefits. This would also mean more landownership by the Service that would require additional funds for management.

This additional demand on funding would limit opportunities for other management options in cooperation with landowners such as restoring prairie, creating wetlands, etc. Landowners who use wildlife compatible practices would not receive an easement payment from the Service to supplement their incomes.

Alternative B (Preferred):

If the Tallgrass Prairie HPA is established, landowners with native prairie would be eligible for easement contracts totaling up to 5,000 acres. Protection of grasslands would be permanent and not subject to changes in the economy, policy, or a change in landownership. The resale value of land may be affected by grassland easements; although from the history of wetland easements, this is difficult to predict. Some land with easements sell for less (which the easement payment compensates for) or the land sells for a competitive price.

Establishing the Tallgrass Prairie Project would enable the Service to work with a wider diversity of landowners. Three to four times as many landowners could be eligible for an easement program than a program restricted to fee title purchases because easements are less expensive. Opportunities for people who own both small and large tracts of land to receive payments would also be increased because the lower cost of easements allow the Service more flexibility and does not restrict the Service to large parcels of land or land near other Service land (WPAs, NWRs). Under an easement program, it may also be more likely that neighboring landowners jointly sign an easement rather than to agree to sell their property to the Service.

The easements would provide additional income for cattle producers as an investment in grazing operations and maintaining the economic diversity of agriculture in South Dakota. These landowners would receive a payment of 25-30 percent of the appraised value of their land. No changes or restrictions would be placed on these grasslands except that the land could not be cultivated and haying could not be done until July 15th. If the landowner was interested, additional programs and wildlife enhancement could be implemented. Potentially, more funding would be available for such enhancement from other grants since money for the Tallgrass Prairie Project would be available for purchasing easements.

Unavoidable Adverse Impacts

No direct or indirect unavoidable adverse impacts to the environment would result from the selection of Alternative B. The identification of an approved boundary for the Tallgrass Prairie Habitat Preservation Area would not result in unavoidable adverse impacts on the physical and biological environment. The selection of an approved boundary does not, by itself, affect any aspect of landownership or values. Once easements are acquired, the Service would prevent incremental adverse impacts, such as degradation and loss of habitat over time, to the lands with their associated native plants and animals.

Irreversible and Irretrievable Commitments of Resources

No irreversible or irretrievable commitments would exist of resources associated with the selection of an approved Tallgrass Prairie Habitat Preservation Area boundary. Under the no-action alternative, if grassland and wetland habitats were not protected and continued to decline, some plant and animal species could disappear over time, causing an irreversible and irretrievable loss. Once lands are acquired and are protected by the Service, irreversible and irretrievable commitments would exist for funds to protect these lands (such as expenditure for fuel and staff for monitoring).

Short-Term Uses Versus Long-Term Productivity

The proposed Tallgrass Prairie Habitat Preservation Area is intended to maintain the long-term biological productivity of the tallgrass prairie ecosystem in South Dakota. The local short-term uses of the environment following acquisition include managing wildlife habitats and maintaining compatible agricultural practices. The resulting long-term productivity includes increased protection of endangered and threatened species and maintenance of biological diversity. The public would gain long-term opportunities for wildlife-dependent recreational activities.

Cumulative Impacts

The conservation easements for protecting the tallgrass prairie ecosystem would have long-term positive cumulative impacts on wildlife habitats within the region of South Dakota. The protection of wildlife habitats on private lands would represent a cumulative benefit to the long-term conservation of migratory birds, endangered species, and biological diversity. The conservation easements would protect a broad spectrum of native habitats and conserve important populations of endangered species and other native plants and animals.

Chapter 5.
Coordination and Environmental Review

Agency Coordination

The proposal for the establishment of the Tallgrass Prairie Habitat Preservation Area, through the authorization of an executive boundary consisting of a project area of 140,860 acres has been discussed with landowners, conservation organizations, Federal, State, and county governments, and other interested groups and individuals.

This Environmental Assessment addresses the acquisition of conservation easements by the Service under the direction of the National Wildlife Refuge System.

Management activities associated with easements may be funded through other sources, such as Migratory Bird Conservation Fund, Wildlife Foundation, Pheasants Forever, Ducks Unlimited, North American Wetland Conservation Association grants, and Partners for Wildlife.

National Environmental Policy Act

As a Federal agency, the U.S. Fish and Wildlife Service must comply with provisions of the National Environmental Policy Act (NEPA). An Environmental Assessment is required under NEPA to evaluate reasonable alternatives that will meet stated objectives and to assess the possible impacts to the human environment. The Environmental Assessment serves as the basis for determining whether implementation of the proposed action would constitute a major Federal action significantly affecting the quality of the human environment. The Environmental Assessment also facilitates the involvement of government agencies and the public in the decision making process.

Other Federal Laws, Regulations, and Executive Orders

In undertaking the proposed action, the Service would comply with a number of Federal laws, Executive Orders, and legislative acts, including:
P   Floodplain Management (Executive Order 11988)
P   Intergovernmental Review of Federal Programs (Executive Order 12372)
P   Protection of Historical, Archaeological, and Scientific Properties (Executive Order 11593)
P   Protection of Wetlands (Executive Order 11990)
P   Management and General Public Use of the National Wildlife Refuge System (Executive Order 12996)
P   Endangered Species Act of 1973, as amended
P   Comprehensive Environmental Responses, Compensation, and Liability Act of 1980
P   Uniform Relocation Assistance and Real Property Acquisition Policy Act of 1970, as amended
P   Refuge Recreation Act, as amended
P   Refuge System Administration Act, as amended
P   National Historic Preservation Act of 1966, as amended.

Distribution and Availability

Copies of this Environmental Assessment were sent to Federal and State legislative delegations, agencies, landowners, private groups, and other interested individuals (see Appendix B). Additional copies of these documents are available at the Sand Lake National Wildlife Refuge office located at 39650 Sand Lake Drive, Columbia, South Dakota, 57433 (telephone 605-885-6320; fax 605-885-6401); and at the U.S. Fish and Wildlife Service's Regional Office in Denver, Colorado (telephone 303-236-8145 extension 658; fax 303-236-4792).

List of Preparers and Reviewers

Authors:

Scott Glup, Supervisory Refuge Operations Specialist, Sand Lake National Wildlife Refuge, Columbia, South Dakota

John F. Esperance, Fish and Wildlife Biologist, Land Acquisition and Refuge Planning Branch, Division of Realty, Refuges and Wildlife, Denver, Colorado

Reviewers:

John Koerner, Refuge Manager, Sand Lake National Wildlife Refuge, Columbia, SD

Harvey Wittmier, Chief, Division of Realty, Refuges and Wildlife, Denver, CO

Maury Wright, Refuge Supervisor, Northern Geographic Ecosystem, Denver, CO

Patrick Russell, Realty Officer, Aberdeen Wetland Acquisition Office, Aberdeen, SD

Acknowledgment:

Jaymee Fojtik, Cartographer, Land Acquisition and Refuge Planning Branch, Division of Realty, Refuges and Wildlife, Denver, Colorado

Barbara Shupe, Writer/Editor, Land Acquisition and Refuge Planning Branch, Division of Realty, Refuges and Wildlife, Denver, Colorado

References

Beauchamp, W.D., Koford, R.R., Nudds, T.D., Clark, R.G. and D.H. Johnson. 1996. Long-term declines in nest success of prairie ducks. J Wild Manage 60(2):247-257.

Cowardin, L.M., Sargeant, A.B., and H.F. Duebbert. 1985. Low waterfowl recruitment in the prairies: the problem, the reasons and the challenge to management. In H. Boyd ed., First Western Hemisphere Waterfowl and Waterbirds Symposium, pgs 16-18.

Dwernychuk, L.W. and D.A. Boag. 1973. Effect of herbicide-induced changes in vegetation on nesting ducks. Canadian Field Naturalist 87:155-165.

Fairlee, Eric E. Thesis in preparation. Floristic and Vegetational analysis of the Hecla sandhills of Northeast South Dakota. M.S. Thesis SDSU Brookings, South Dakota.

Gerard, P.W. 1995. Agricultural practices, farm policy and the conservation of biological diversity. National Biological Service Technical Report Series, Biological Science Report 4:28pp.

Grue, C.E., Tome, M.W., Swanson, G.A., Borthwick, S.M. and L.R. DeWeese. 1988. Agricultural chemicals and the quality of prairie-pothole wetlands for adult and juvenile waterfowl-what are the concerns? Nat Symposium on Protection of Wetlands from Agricultural Impacts, CSU, Ft. Collins, CO.

HAPET- Habitat and Population Evaluation Team, USFWS. 1996. Waterfowl breeding pair distributions in the prairie pothole region of North and South Dakota (GIS map). Bismarck, North Dakota.

Hartwig, N.L. and J.K. Hall. 1980. Influencing the action of herbicides: runoff losses. Crops and Soil Magazine, October:14-16.

Kantrud, H.A. and K.F. Higgins. 1992. Nest and nest site characteristics of some ground-nesting, nonpasserine birds of northern grasslands. Prairie Nat 24(2):67-84.

Kantrud, H.A., Krapu, G.L. and G.A. Swanson. 1989. Prairie basin wetlands of the Dakotas: a community profile. USFWS Biol Rep 85(7.28). 116pgs.

Klett, A.T., Shaffer, T.L. and D.H. Johnson. 1988. Duck nest success in the prairie pothole region. J Wildl Management 52:431-440.

Larson, Gary. Personal interview with Service employee. June 1999

Owens, R. and M.T. Myers. 1972. Effects of agriculture upon populations of native passerine birds of an Alberta fescue grassland. Can J Zool. 51: 697-713.

Pimentel, D., Acquay, H., Biltonen, M., Rice, P., Silva, M., Nelson, J., Lipner, V., Giordano, S., Horowitz, A., and M. D'Amore. 1992. Environmental and economic costs of pesticide use. BioScience 42(10): 33-43.

Sauer, J.R., Peterjohn, B.G., Schwartz, S., and J.E. Hines. 1995. The grassland bird homepage. Ver 95.0 Patuxtent Wildlife Research Center. Laurel, MD.

Sovada, M.A., Sargeant, A.B. and J.W. Grier. 1995. Differential effects of coyotes and red foxes on duck nest success. J Wildl Manage. 59(1):1-9.

USDA, Soil Conservation Service. 1936. Map of South Dakota Erosion and Land-Use Conditions. Brown and Marshall Counties, SD.

USFWS, Environmental Assessment of the management of upland habitats on Sand Lake Wetland Management District, South Dakota. May 1, 1994.

Appendix A.
List of Scientific
Names Used in Text

Plant Species

alpine rush	*Juncus alpinoarticulatus*
big bluestem	*Andropogon gerardii*
grass-leaved rush	*Juncus marginatus*
great plains ladies tresses	*Spiranthes magnicamporum*
green needlegrass	*Stipa viridula*
little bluestem	*Schizachyrium scoparium*
Indian grass	*Sorghstrum nutans*
lead plant	*Amorpha canescens*
Maximillian's sunflower	*Helianthus maximiliana*
meadowsweet	*Spirea alba*
moonwort	*Botrichium simplex*
needle-and-thread	*Stipa comata*
nodding ladies'-tresses	*Spiranthes Cermia*
paspalum	*Paspalum setaceum var. stramineum*
pinweed	*Lechea stricta*
porcupine grass	*Stipa spartea*
prairie cordgrass	*Spartina pectinata*
prairie coneflower	*Echinacea angustifolia*
prairie dunewort	*Botrychium campestre*
prairie loosestrife	*Lysimachia quadriflora*
prairie sandreed	*Calamovilfa longifolia*
sand bluestem	*Andropogon hallii*
sedge	*Lipocarpa mancrantha*
smooth goosefoot	*Chenopodium subglabrum*
western prairie fringed orchid	*Platanthera Praeclara*
western wheatgrass	*Pascopyrum smithii*

Bird/Insect Species

black terns	*Chlidonias niger*
bobolinks	*Dolichonyx orysivorus*
chestnut-collared longspurs	*Calcarius ornatus*
Dakota skipper	*Hesperia dacotae*
grasshopper sparrows	*Ammodramus savannarum*
Iowa Skipper	*Atrytone arogos iowa*
Powesheik. Skipper	*Oarisma powesheik*
marbled godwits	*Limosa fedoa*
marsh wren	*Telmatodytes palustis*
Ottoe Skipper	*Hesperia ottoe*
phalaropes	*Steganopus tricolor*
regal fritillary	*Speyeria idalia*
savannah sparrows	*Passerculus sandwichensis*
sedge wrens	*Cistothorus platensis*
song sparrows	*Melospiza melodia*
willets	*Catoptrophorus semipalmatus*
yellowthroats	*Geothlypis trichas*

Appendix B.
Mailing List

Federal Officials
P   U.S. Representative John Thune
P   U.S. Senator Thomas A. Daschle
P   U.S. Senator Tim Johnson

Federal Agencies
P   USDA/Farm Service Agency
P   USDA/Natural Resources Conservation Service

State Officials
P   Governor William J. Janklow
P   State Representative H. Paul Dennert
P   State Representative Steve Cutler
P   State Representative Duane Sutton

State Agencies
P   SD Game, Fish and Parks Department

Groups
P   The Nature Conservancy

Individuals

Appendix C.
Endangered, Threatened, and Candidate Species

Tallgrass Prairie Habitat Preservation Project Area
(Updated September 1999)

Species	Certainty of Occurrence	Group	Status
Curlew, Eskimo	Extremely Rare	Bird	E
Orchid, Western Prairie Fringed	Possible	Plant	T
Eagle, Bald**	Known	Bird	T
Topeka Shiner	Known	Fish	E

The counties indicated for the Western prairie fringed orchid are counties with potential habitat. Currently, no known populations exist of this species in South Dakota. Status surveys have been completed for the orchid in South Dakota. However, because of the ecology of this species, a possibility exists that plants may be overlooked.

** Bald eagles have successfully nested in Gregory, Brown, Yankton, Bon Homme, Spink, Charles Mix, Union, Roberts, Sanborn, Hutchinson, and Meade Counties.

T - Threatened
E - Endangered

Sand Lake National Wildlife Refuge
39650 Sand Lake Drive
Columbia, SD 57433
605/885 6320
r6rw_sdl@fws.gov

U. S. Fish and Wildlife Service
http://www.fws.gov

For Refuge Information
1 800/344 WILD

January 2000

Ladies Tresses. 8*Keith Frankki*